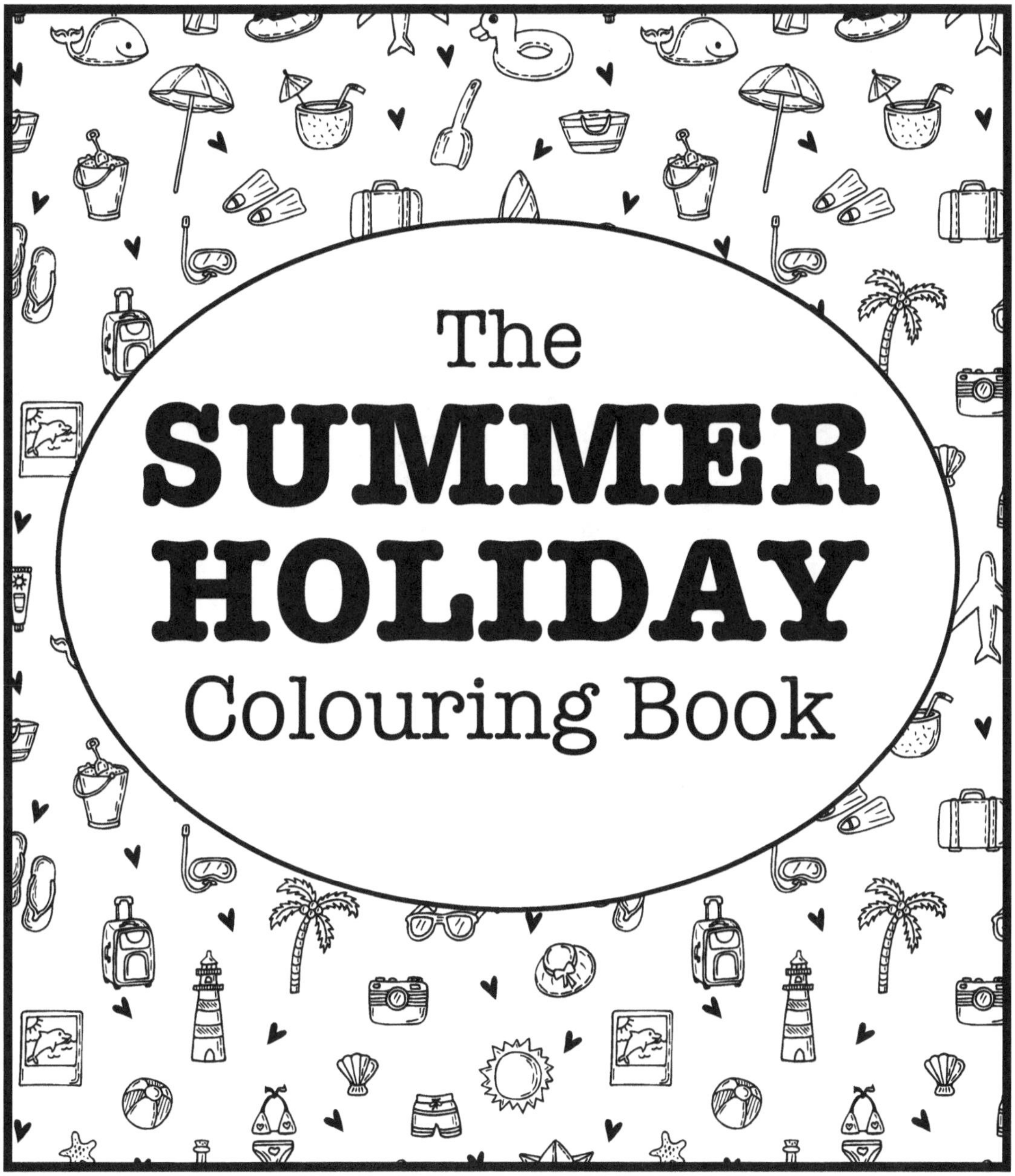

The

SUMMER HOLIDAY

Colouring Book

First published in 2016 by Kyle Craig Publishing

Design: Elizabeth James, Julie Anson, Alison McNicol, Shutterstock, Inc.

ISBN: 978-1-78595-151-0

A CIP record for this book is available from the British Library.

A Kyle Craig Publication

www.kyle-craig.com

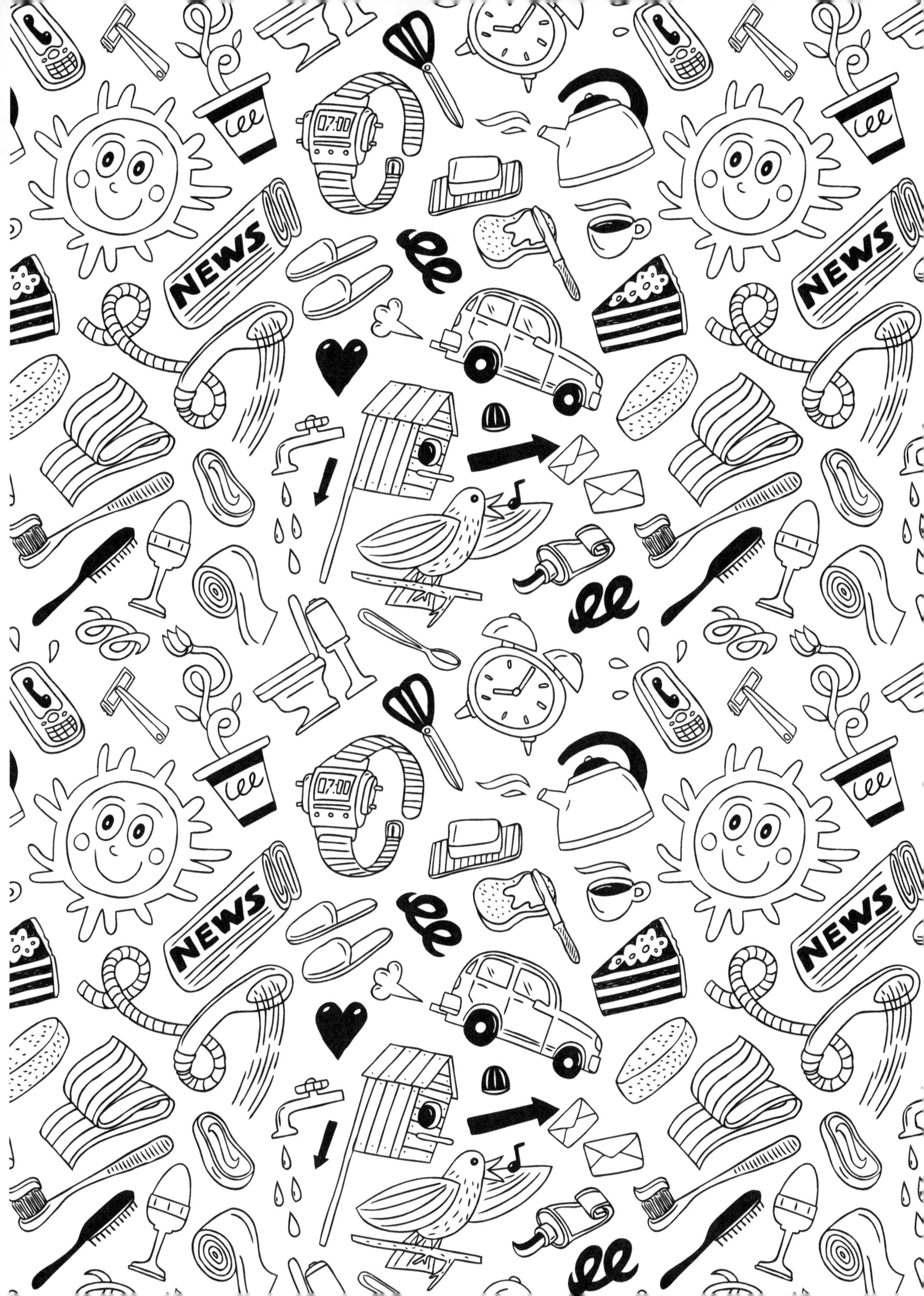
NEWS
07:00

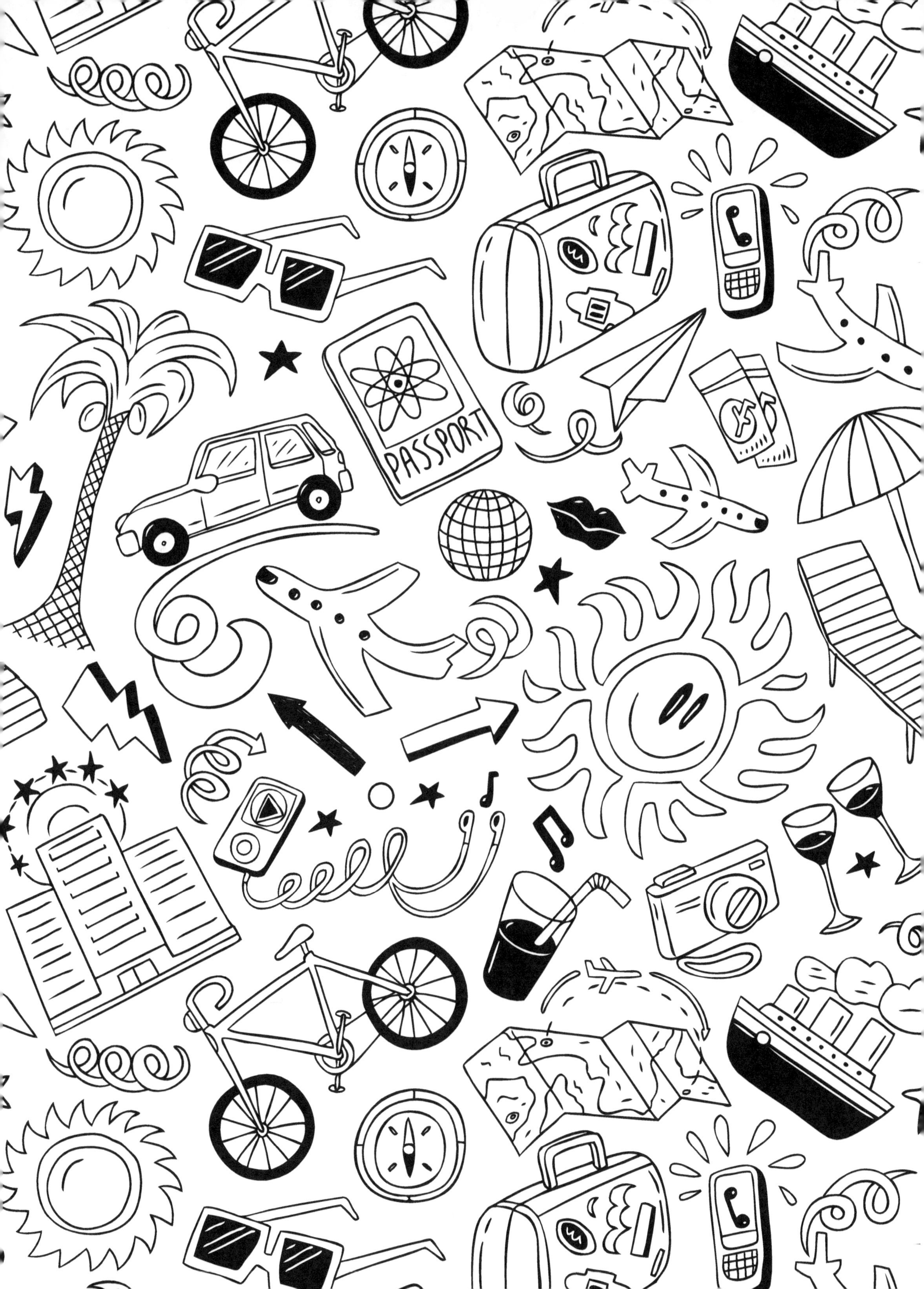
PASSPORT

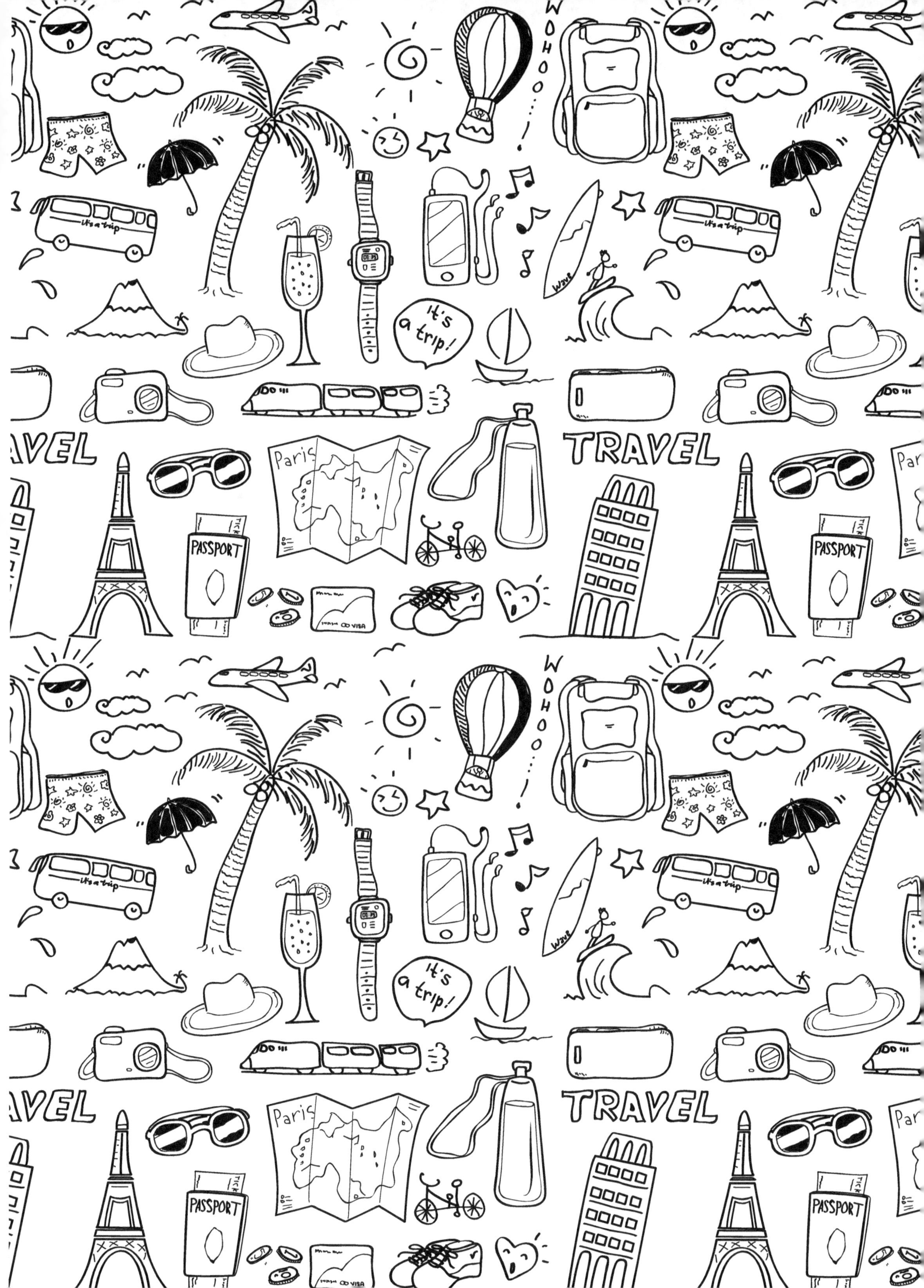
WOHOO...!
it's a trip
it's a trip!
Wave
TRAVEL
Paris
PASSPORT
VISA

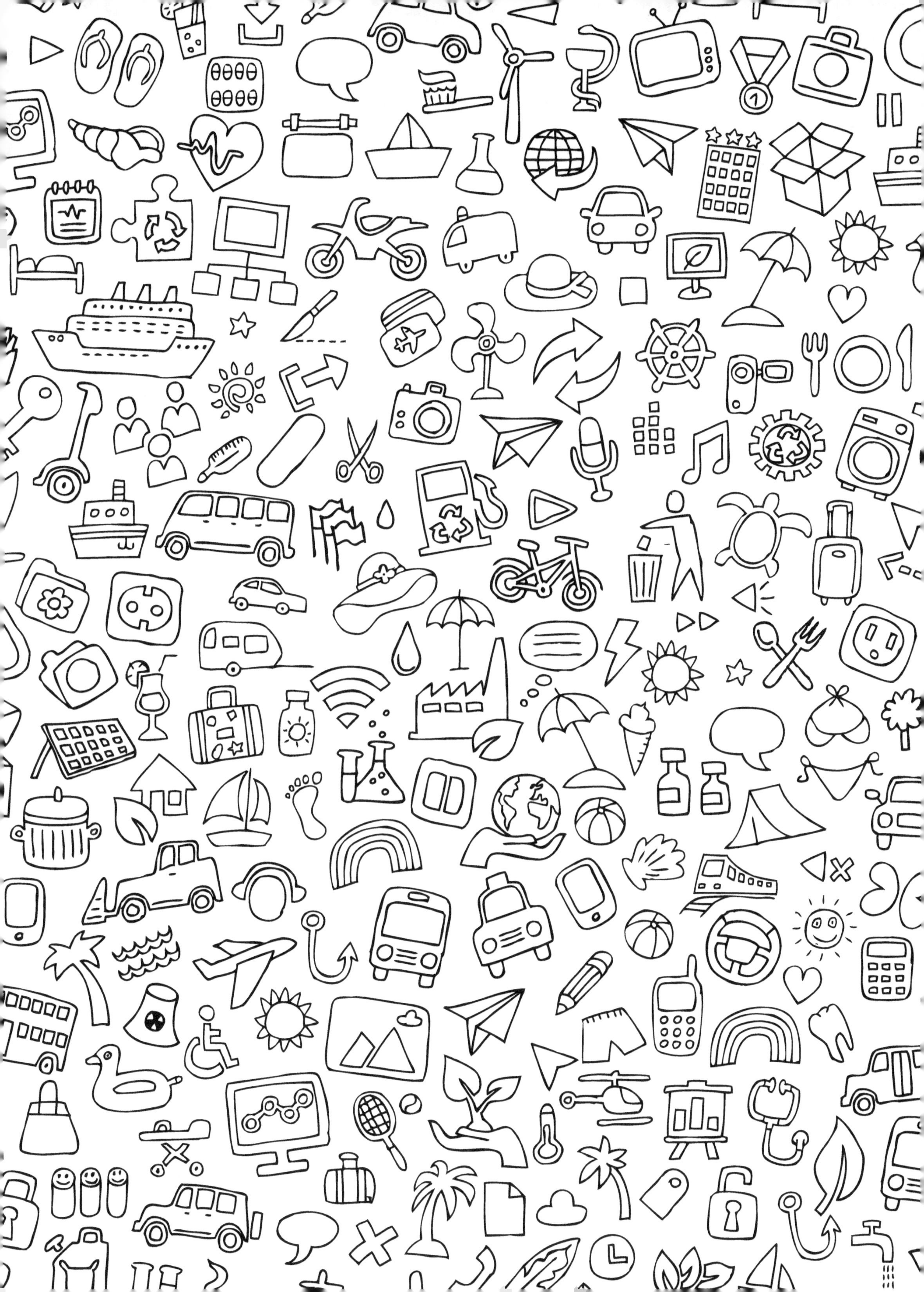

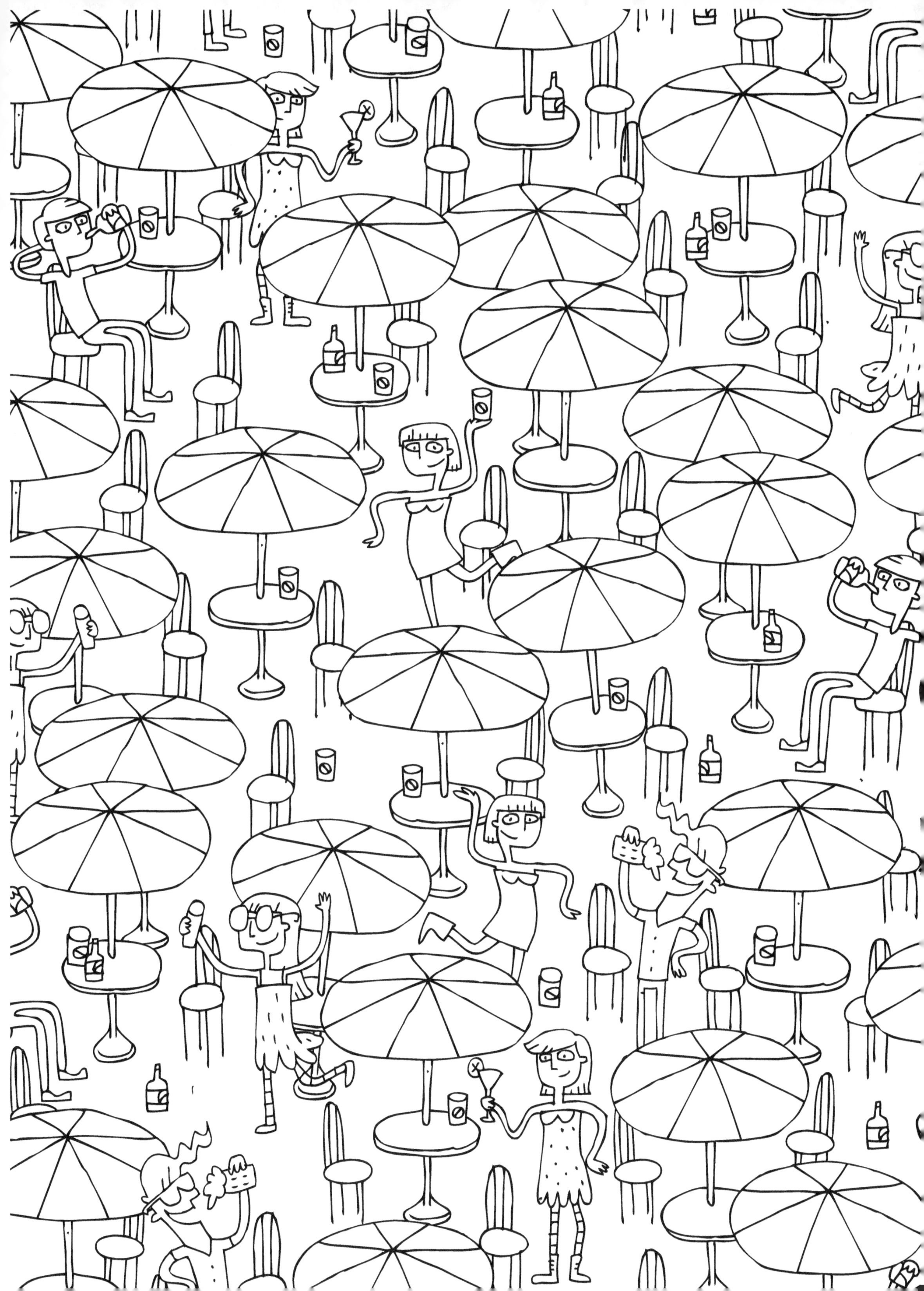

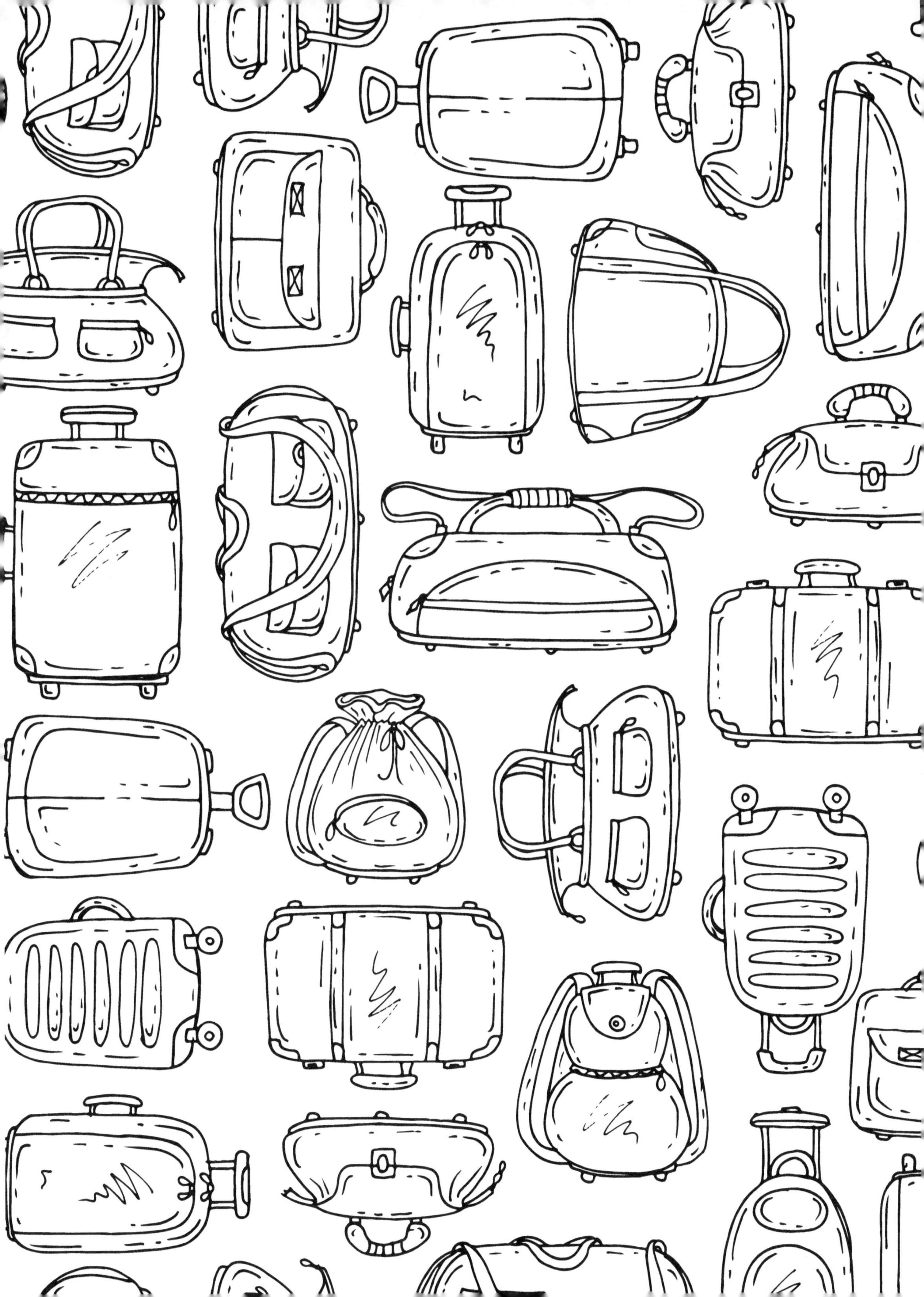

SUN
SUN

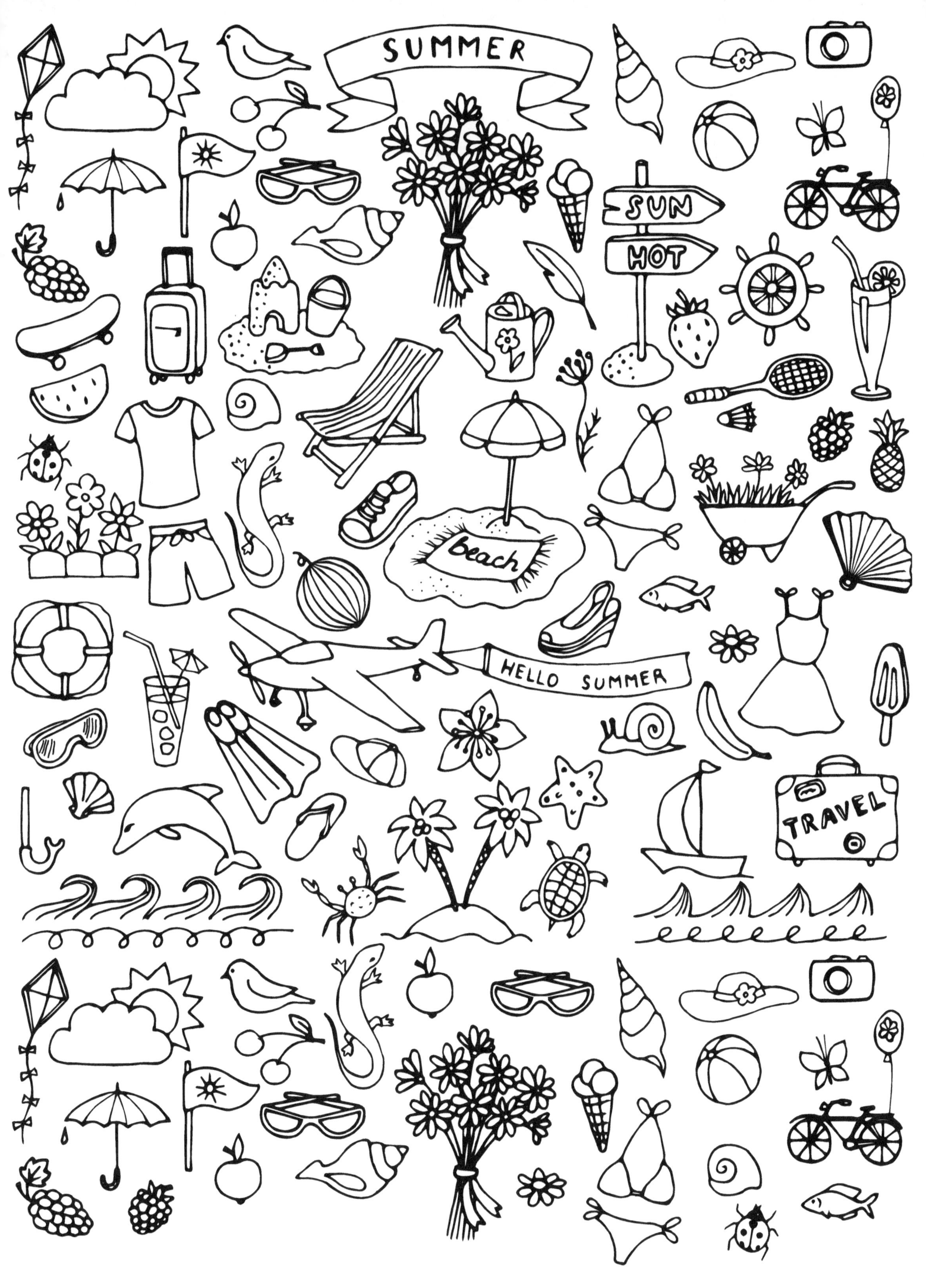
SUMMER
SUN
HOT
beach
HELLO SUMMER
TRAVEL

GREECE
GREECE
GREECE
GREECE
GREECE

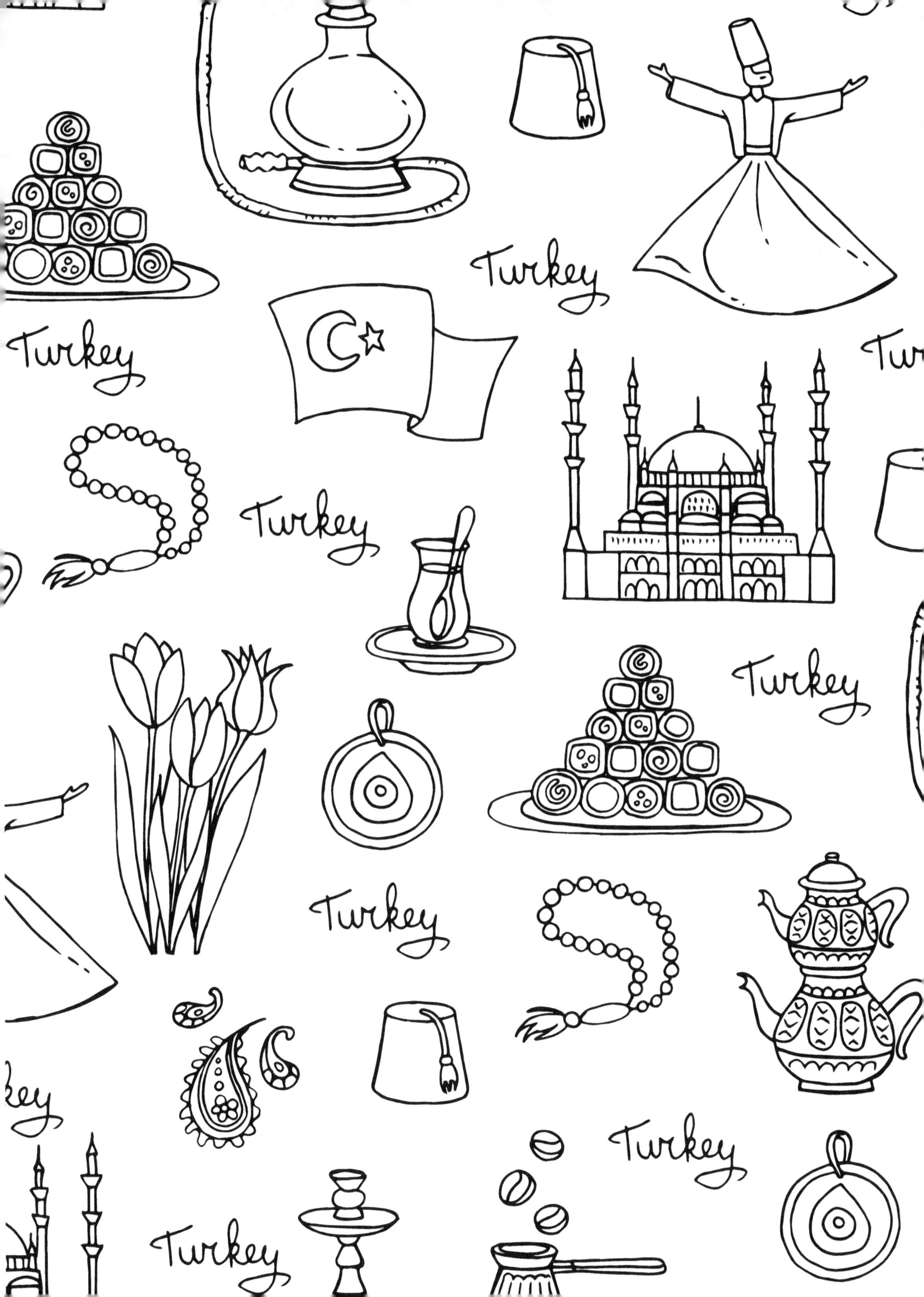
Turkey
Turkey
Tur
Turkey
Turkey
Turkey
key
Turkey
Turkey

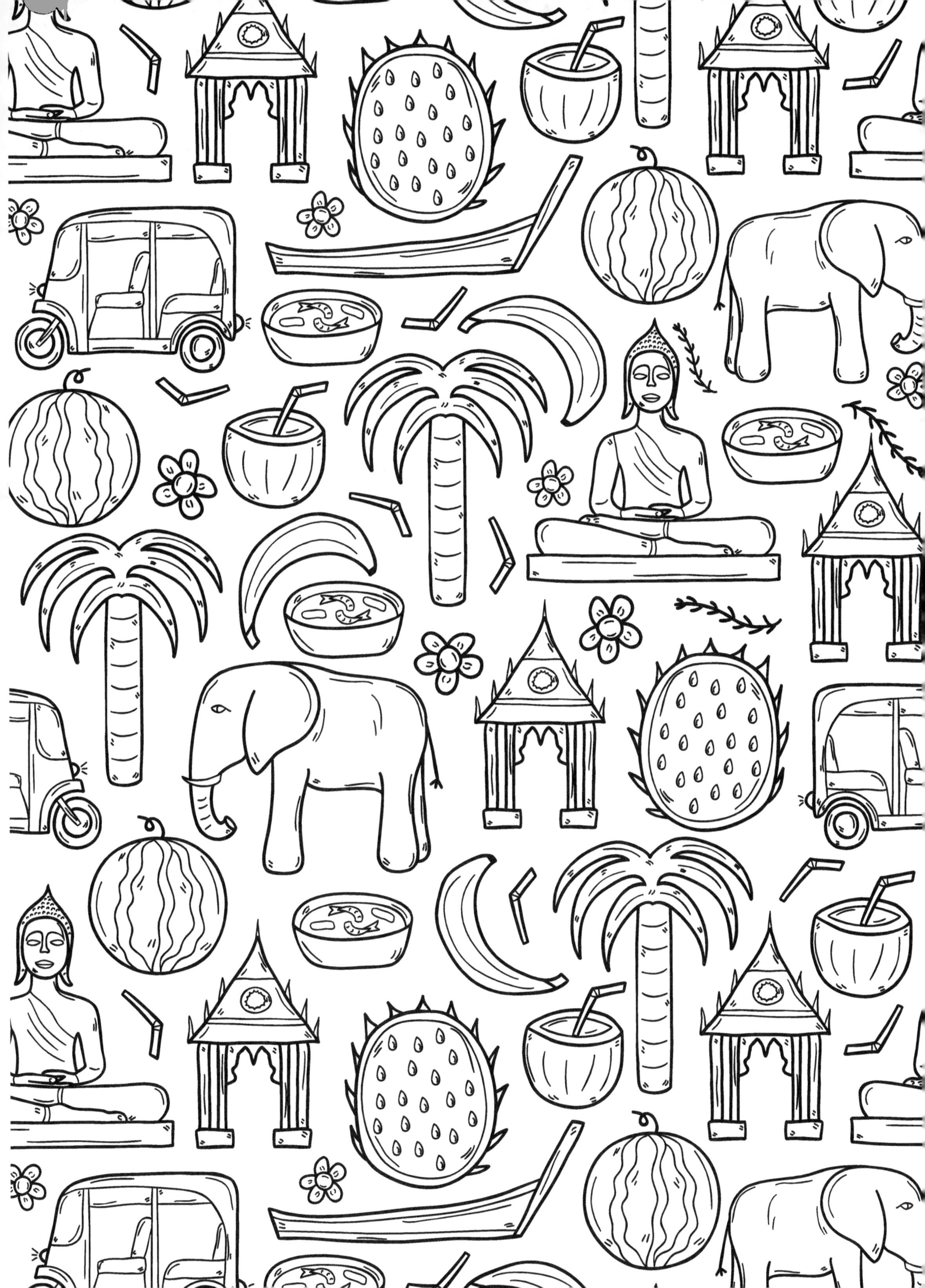

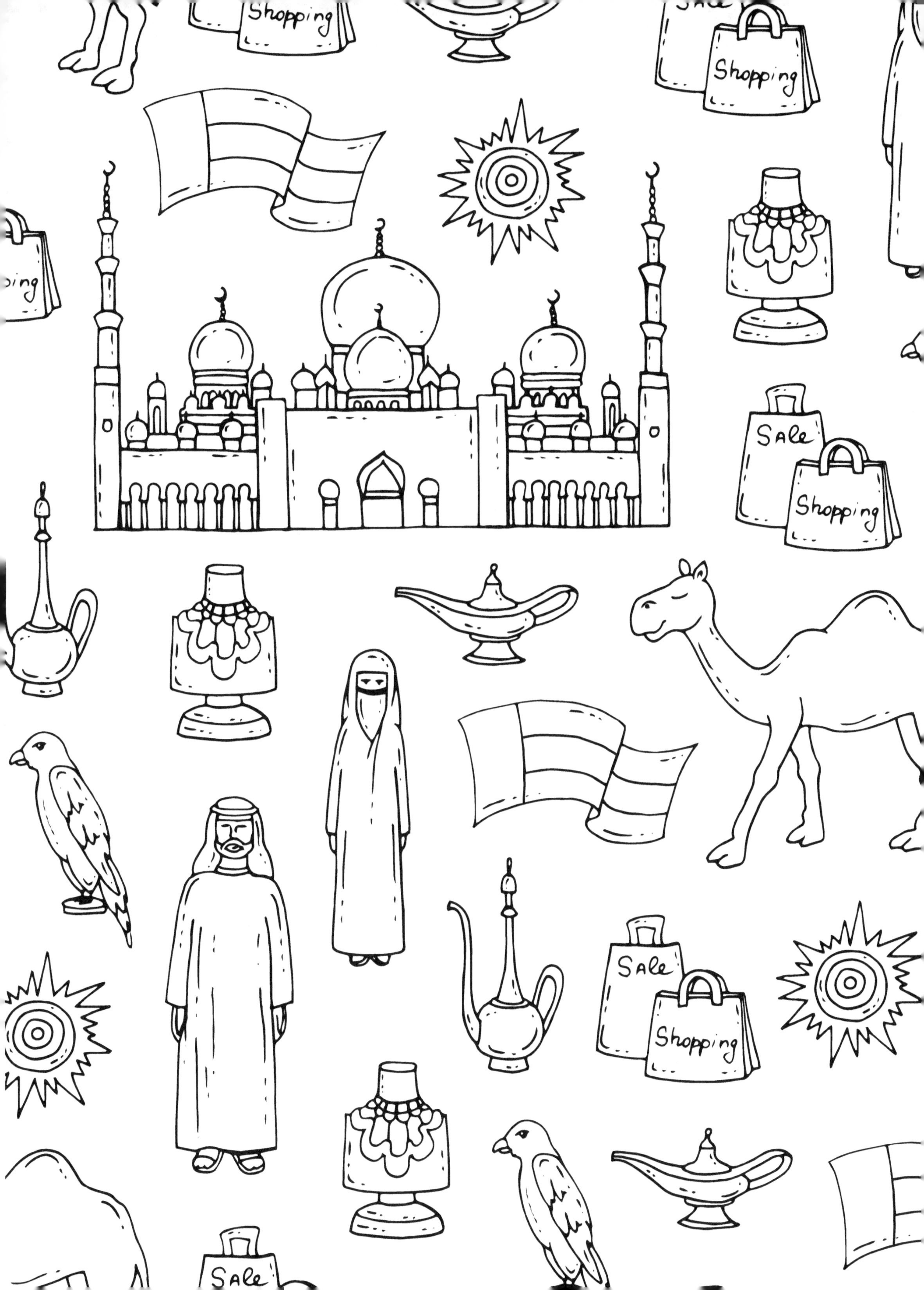
Shopping
Shopping
ping
Sale
Shopping
Sale
Shopping
Sale

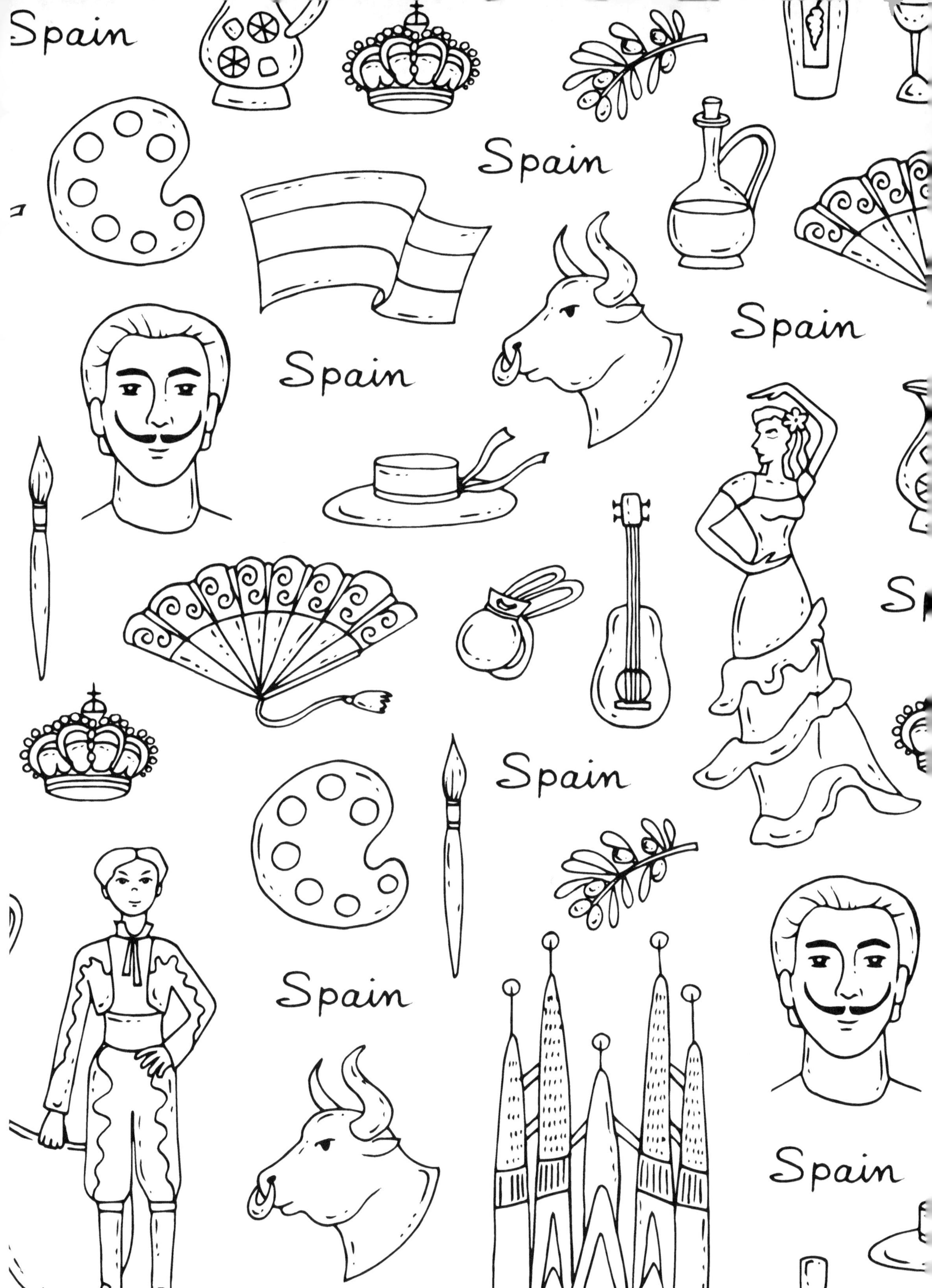
Spain
Spain
Spain
Spain
Spain
Spain
Spain

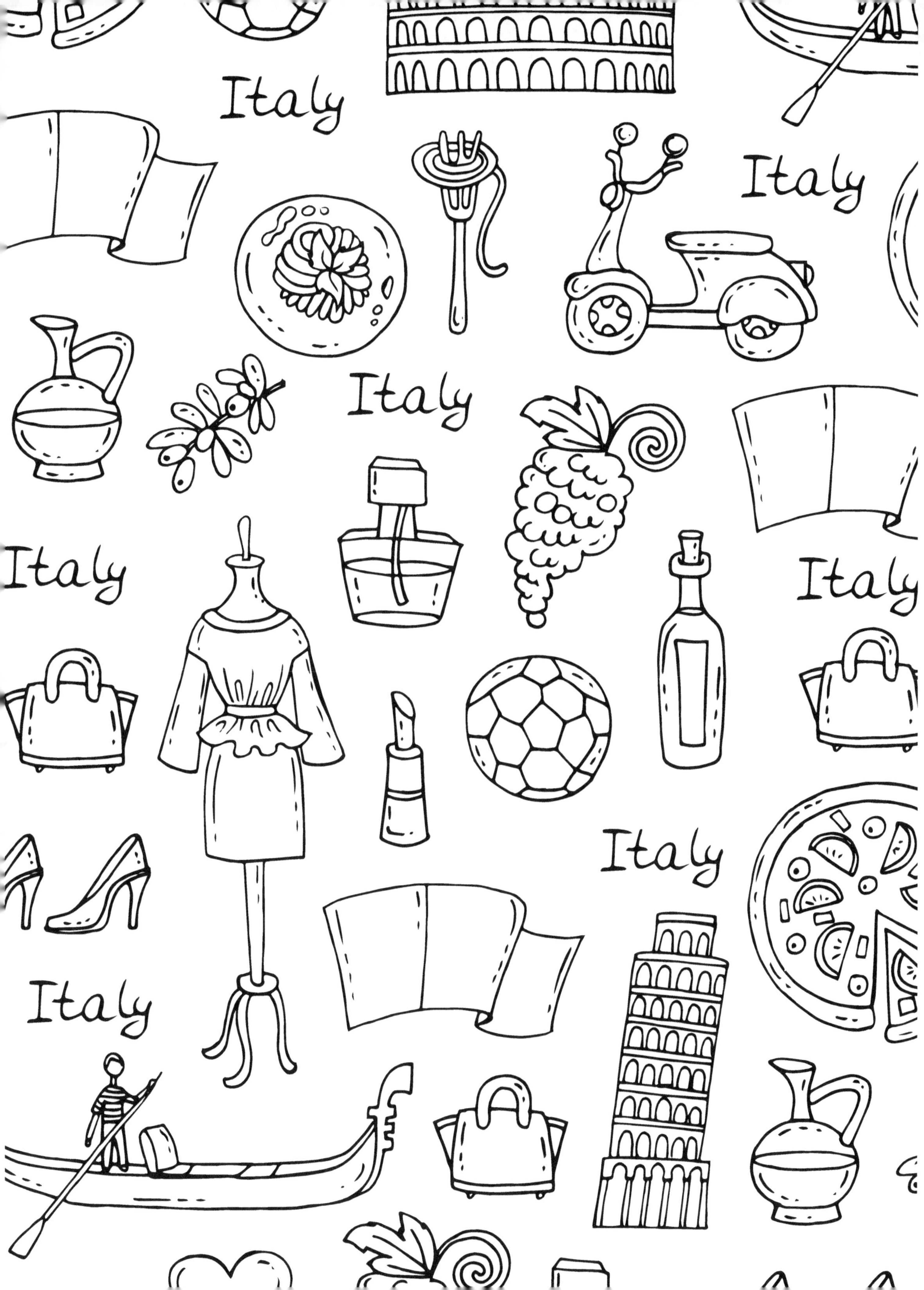
Italy
Italy
Italy
Italy
Italy
Italy
Italy

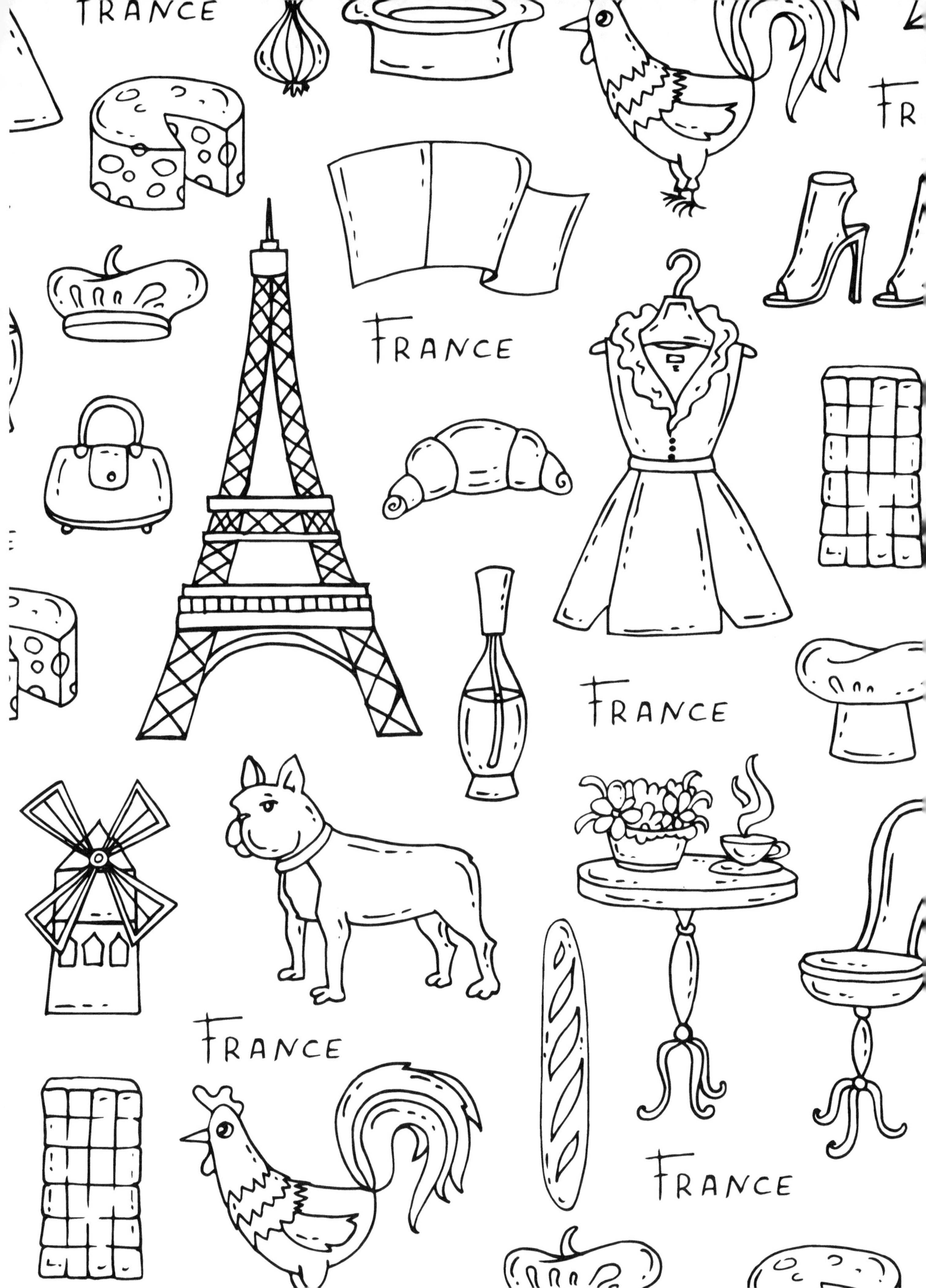
FRANCE
FRANCE
FRANCE
FRANCE

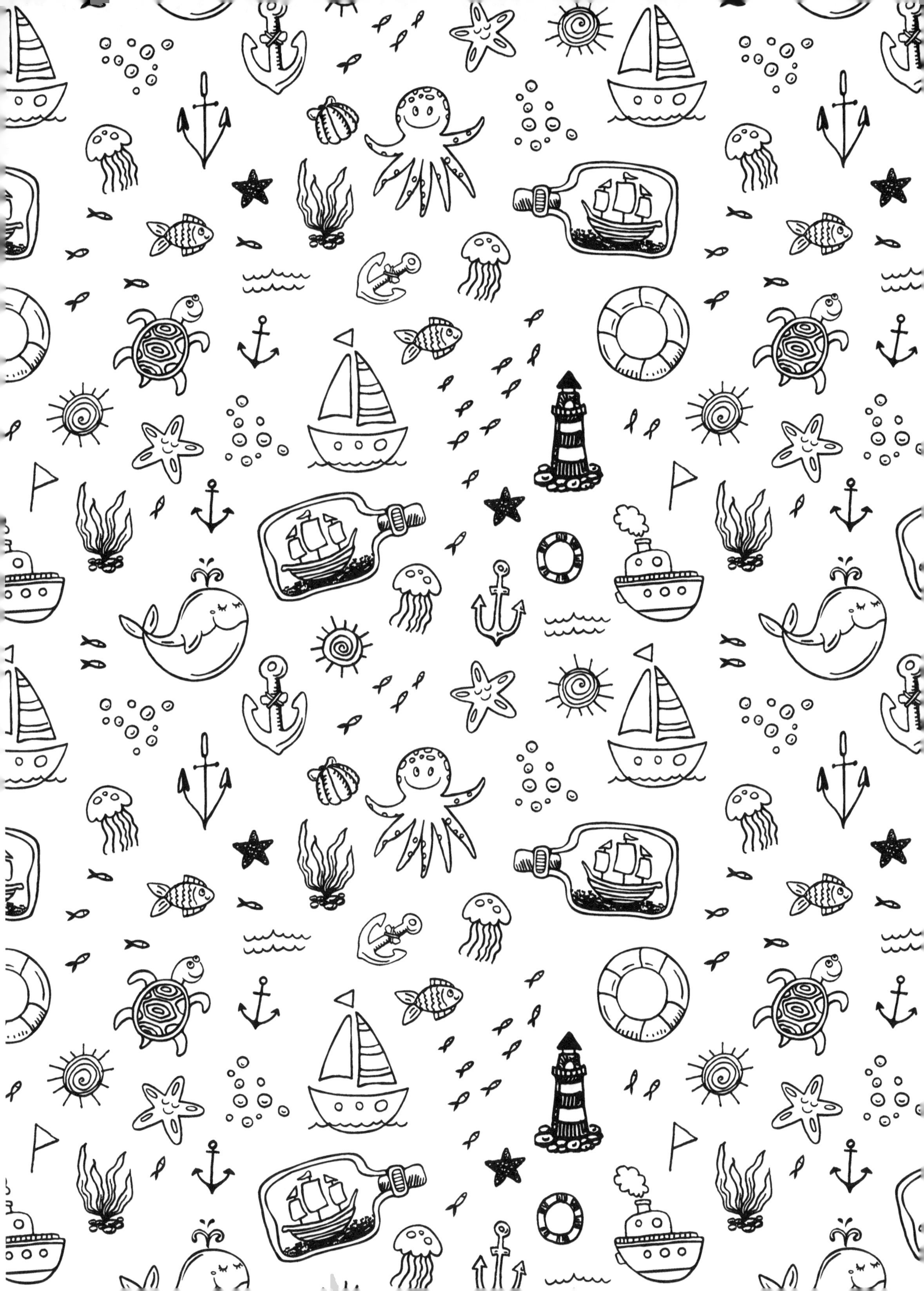

United Kingdom
Uni
United Kingdom
ited Kingdom
TELEPHONE
United Kingdom

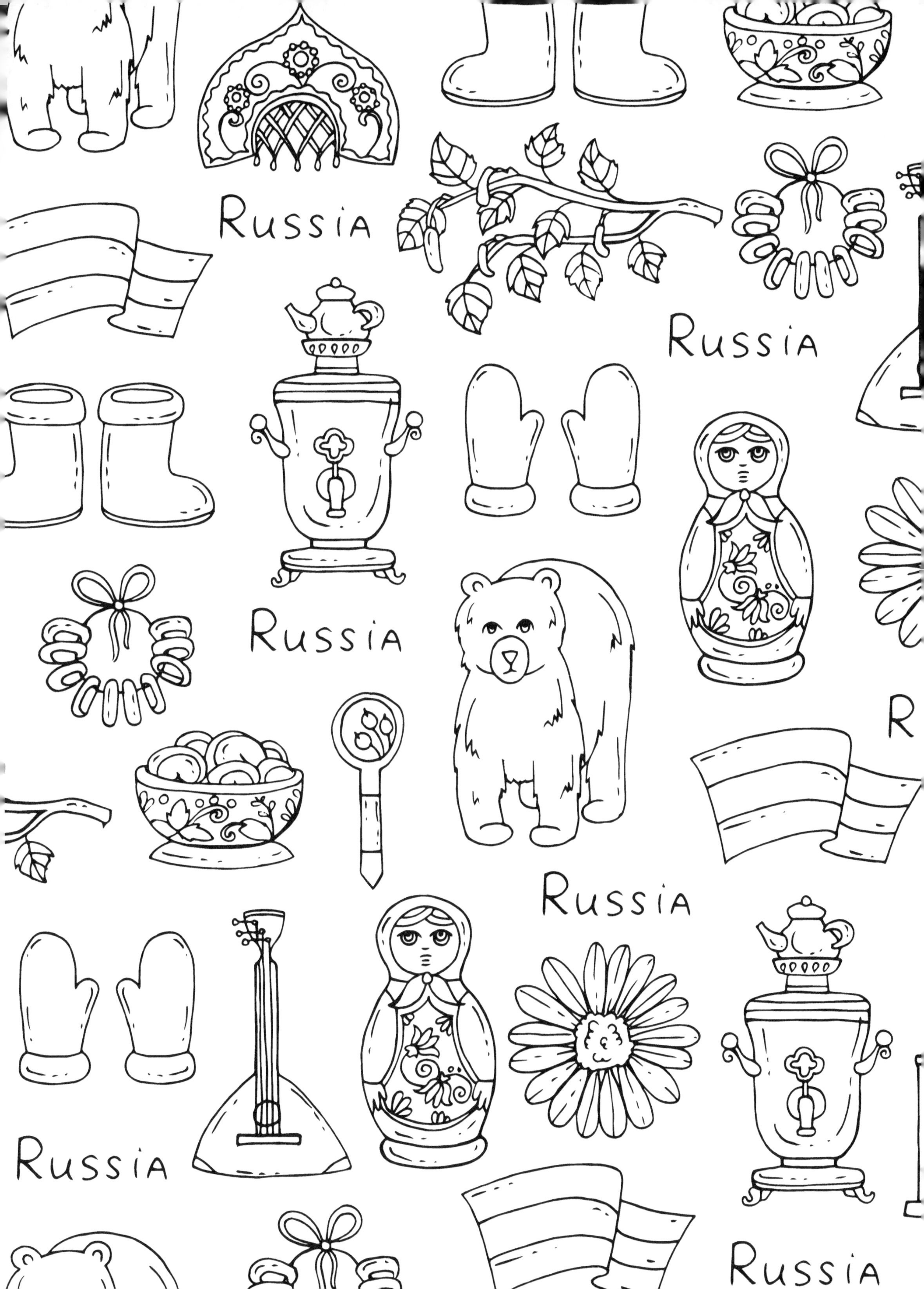
Russia
Russia
Russia
Russia
Russia
Russia

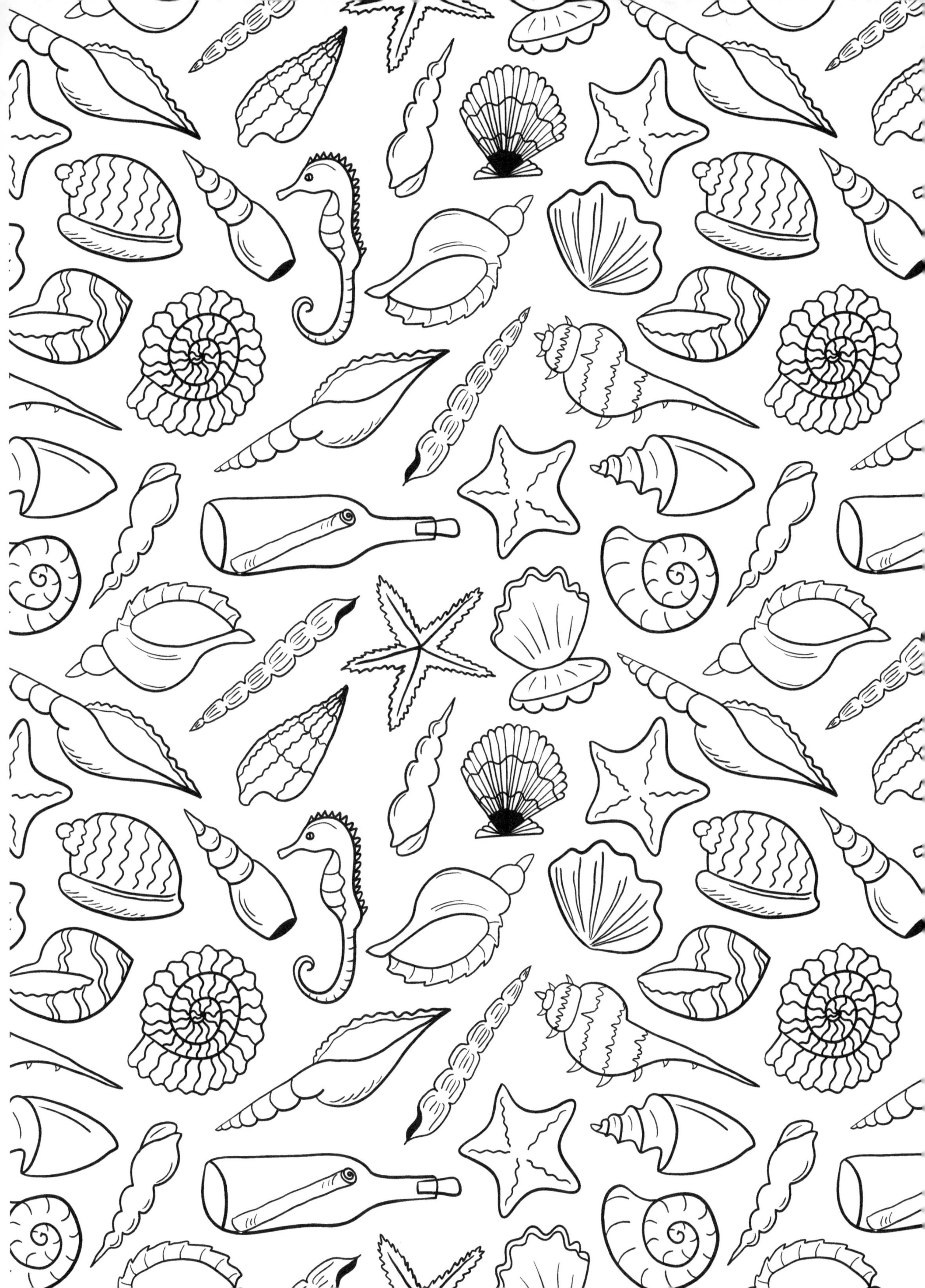

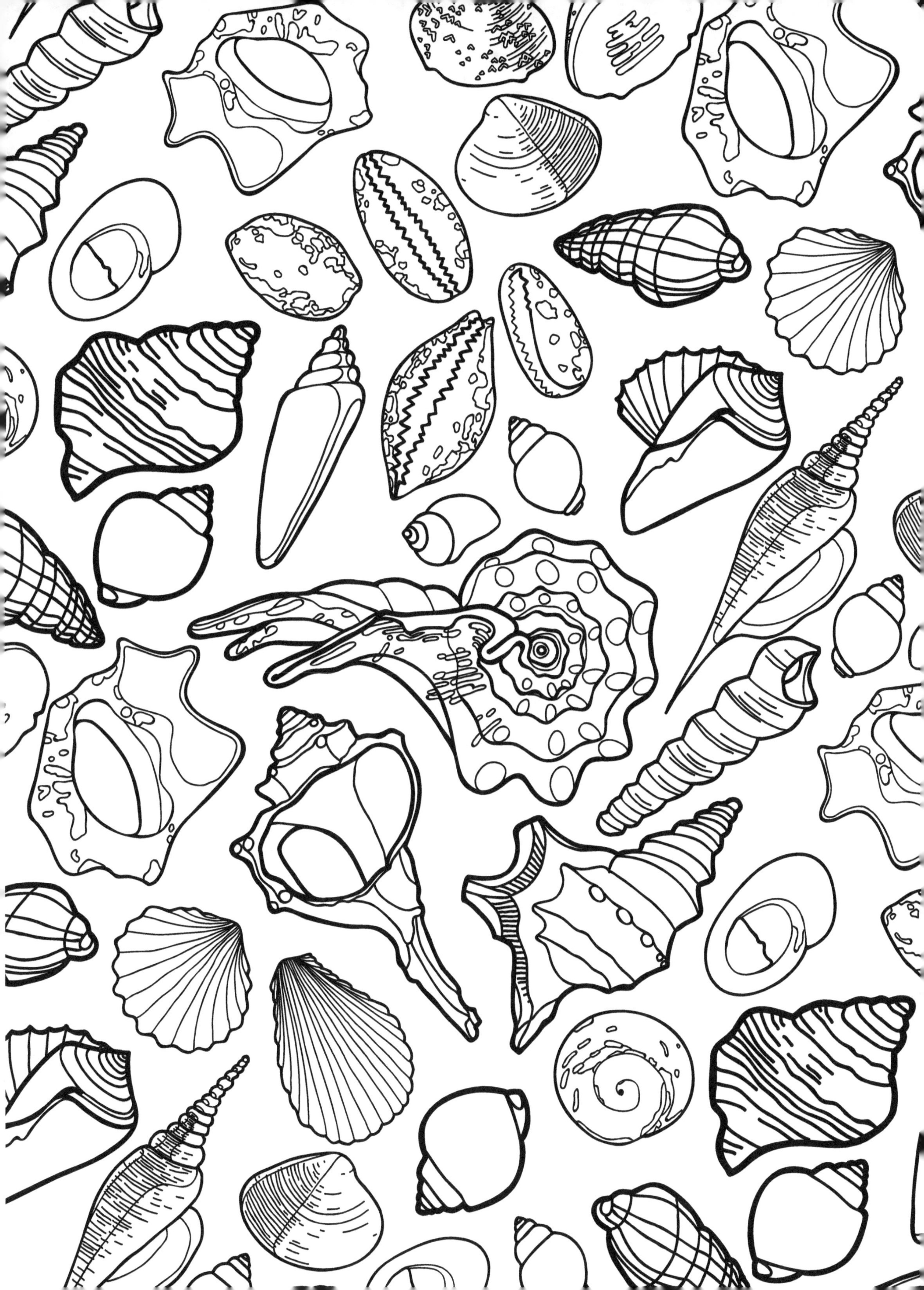

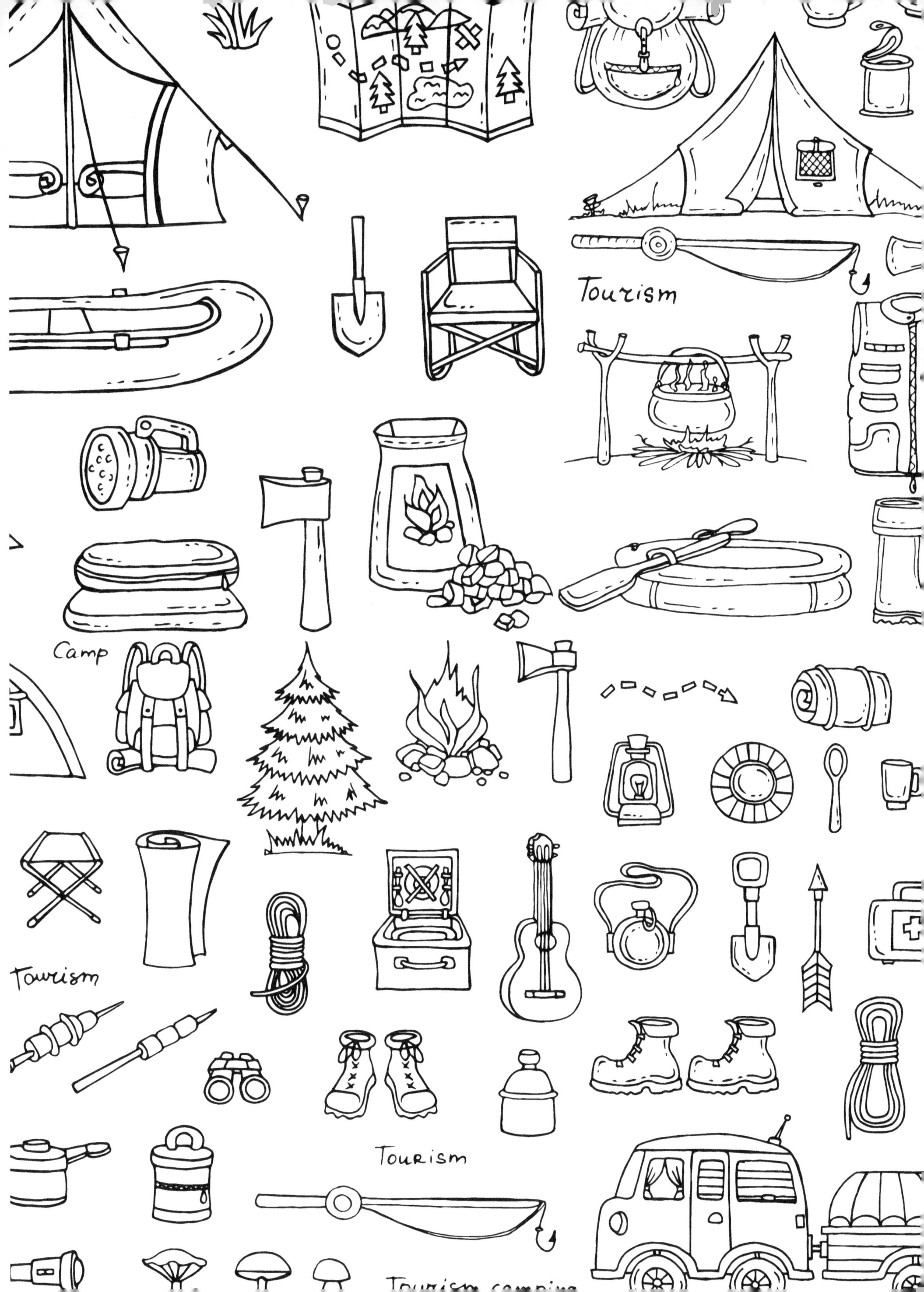
Tourism
Camp
Tourism
Tourism

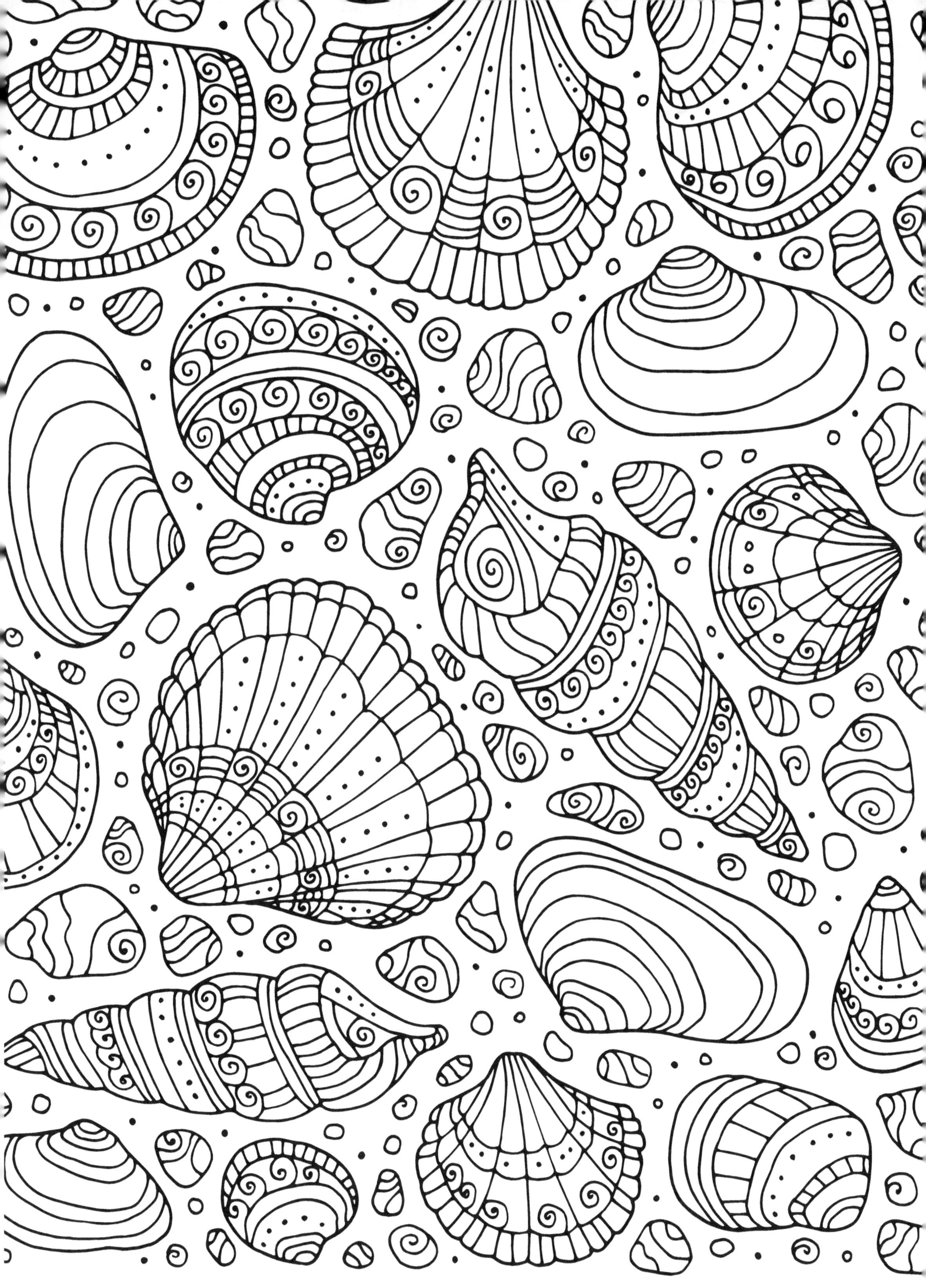

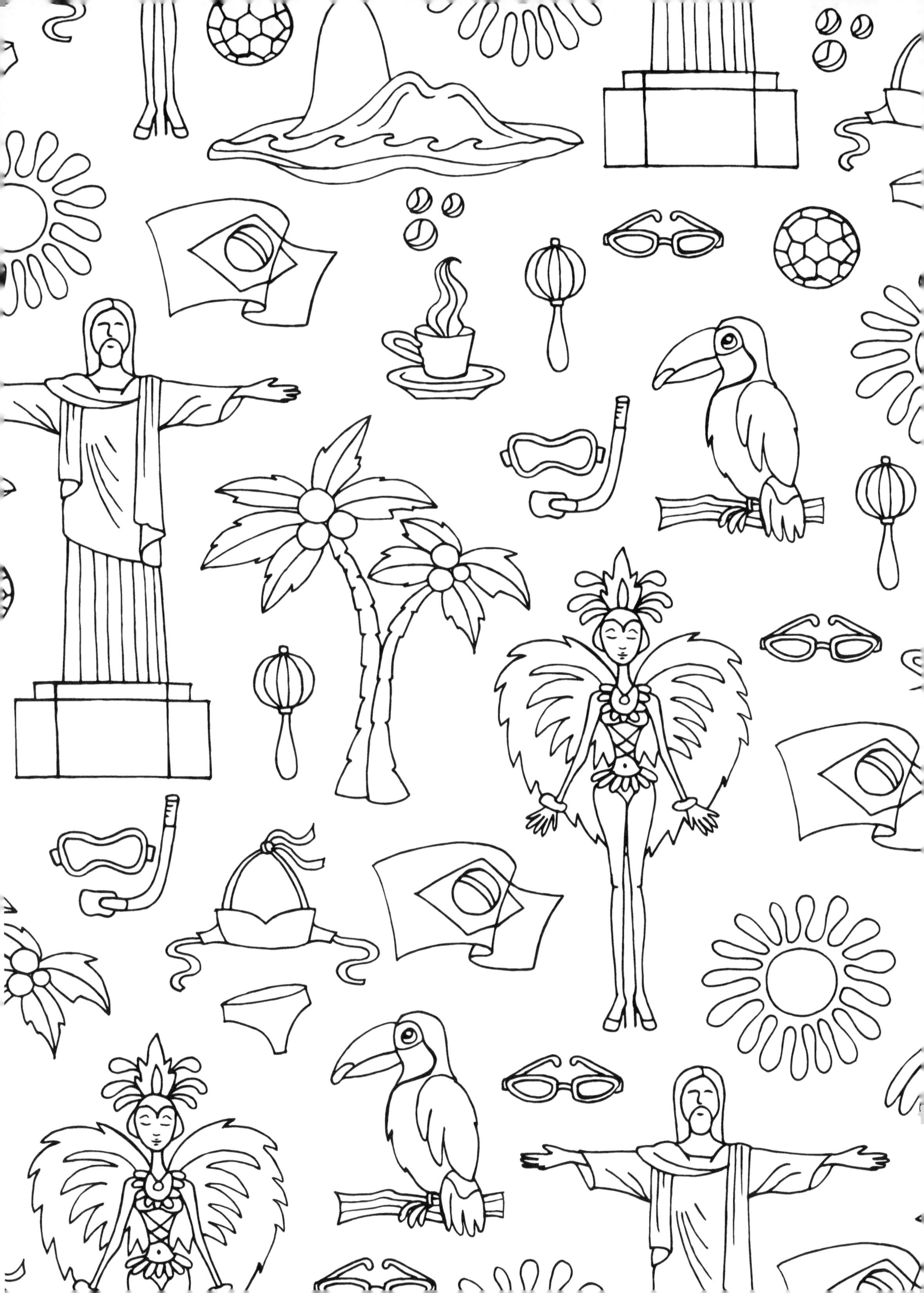

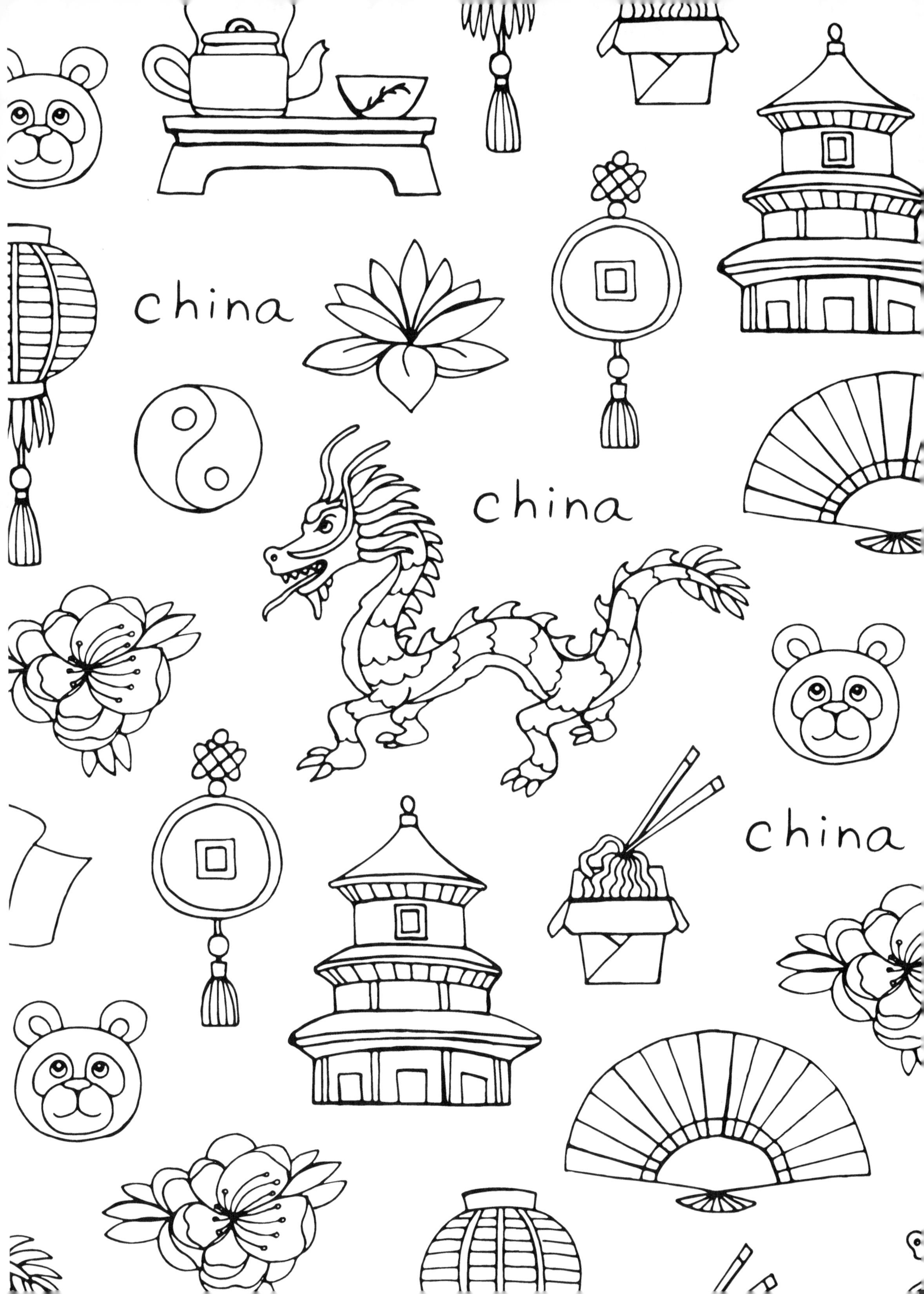
china
china
china

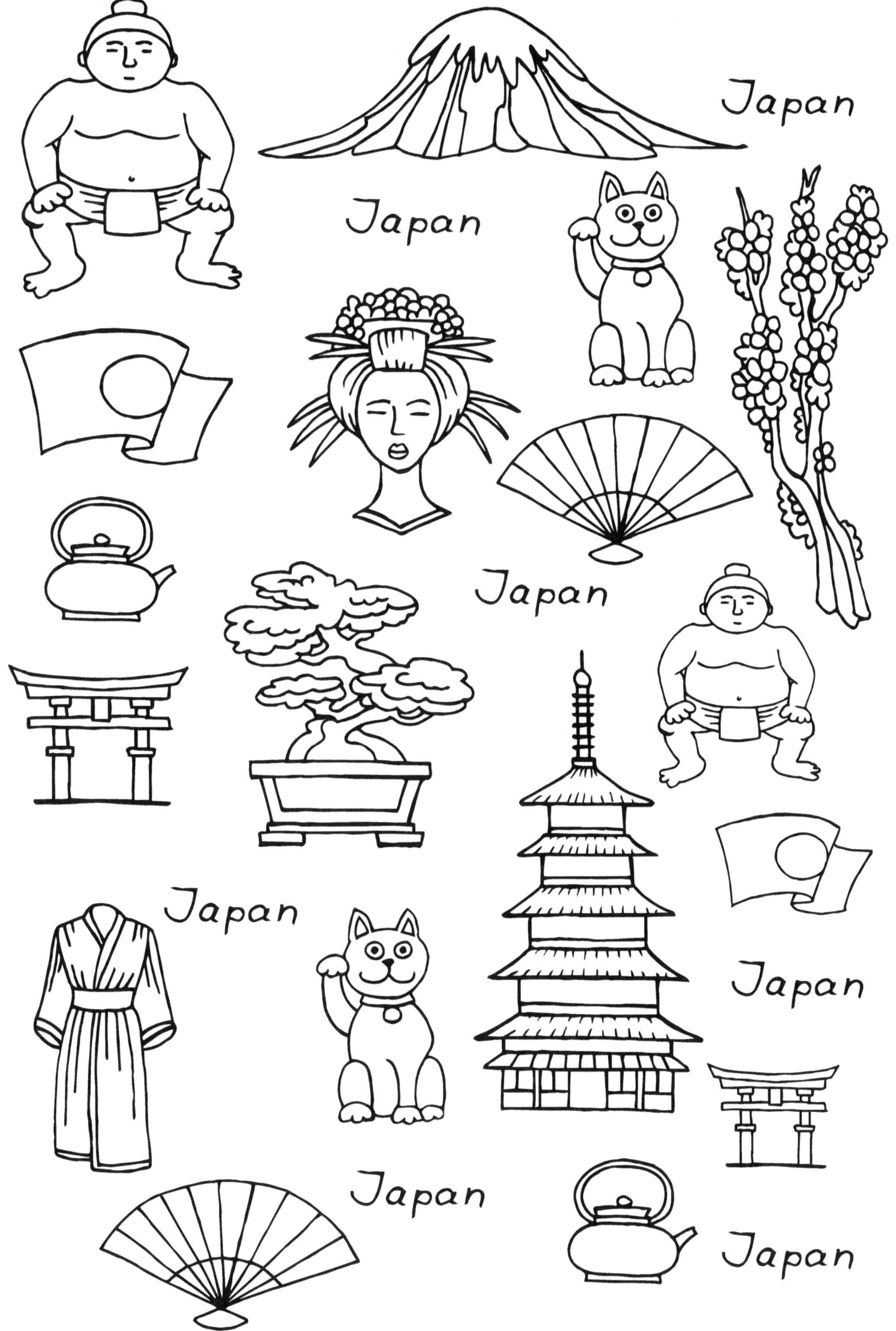
Japan
Japan
Japan
Japan
Japan
Japan
Japan

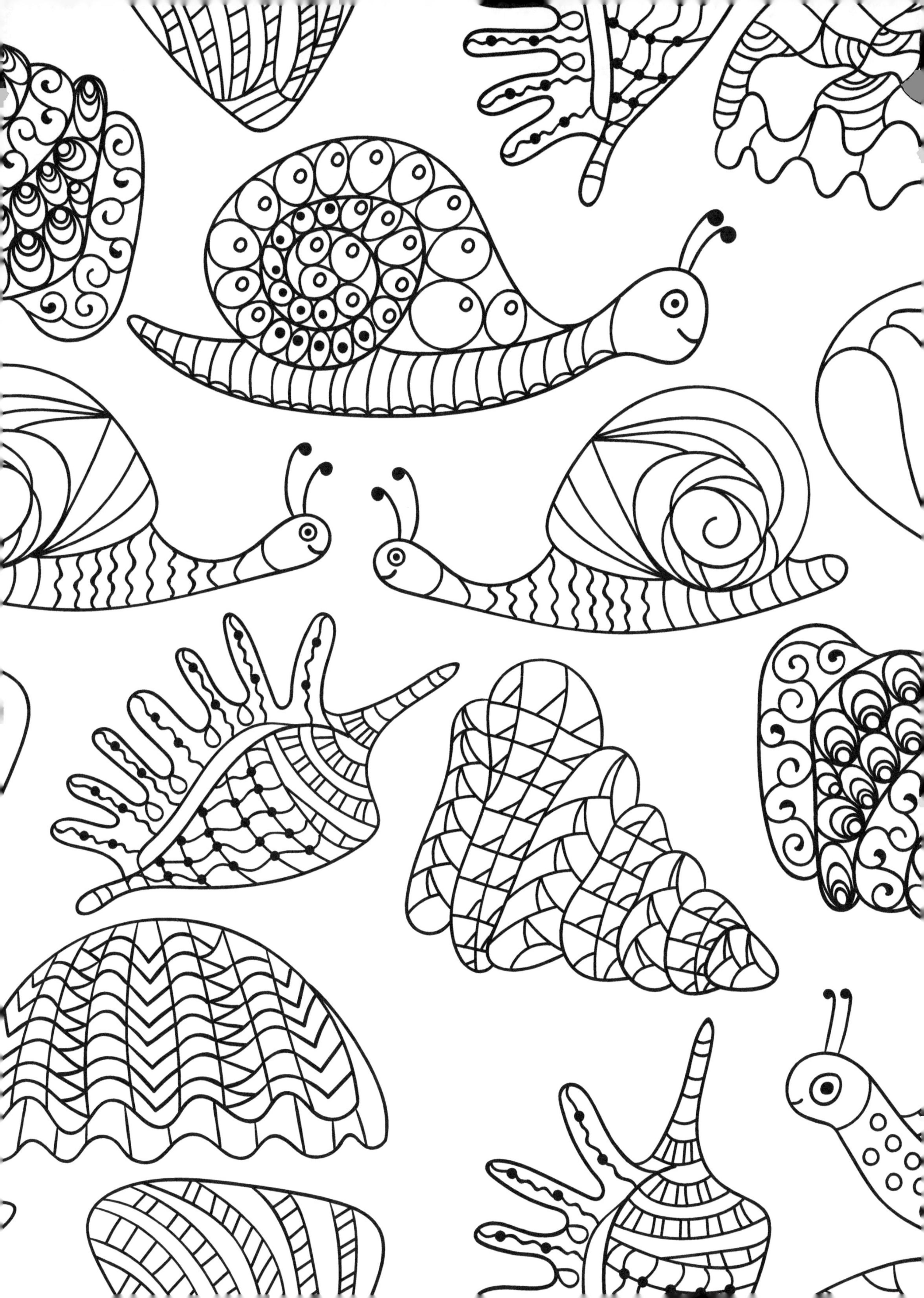

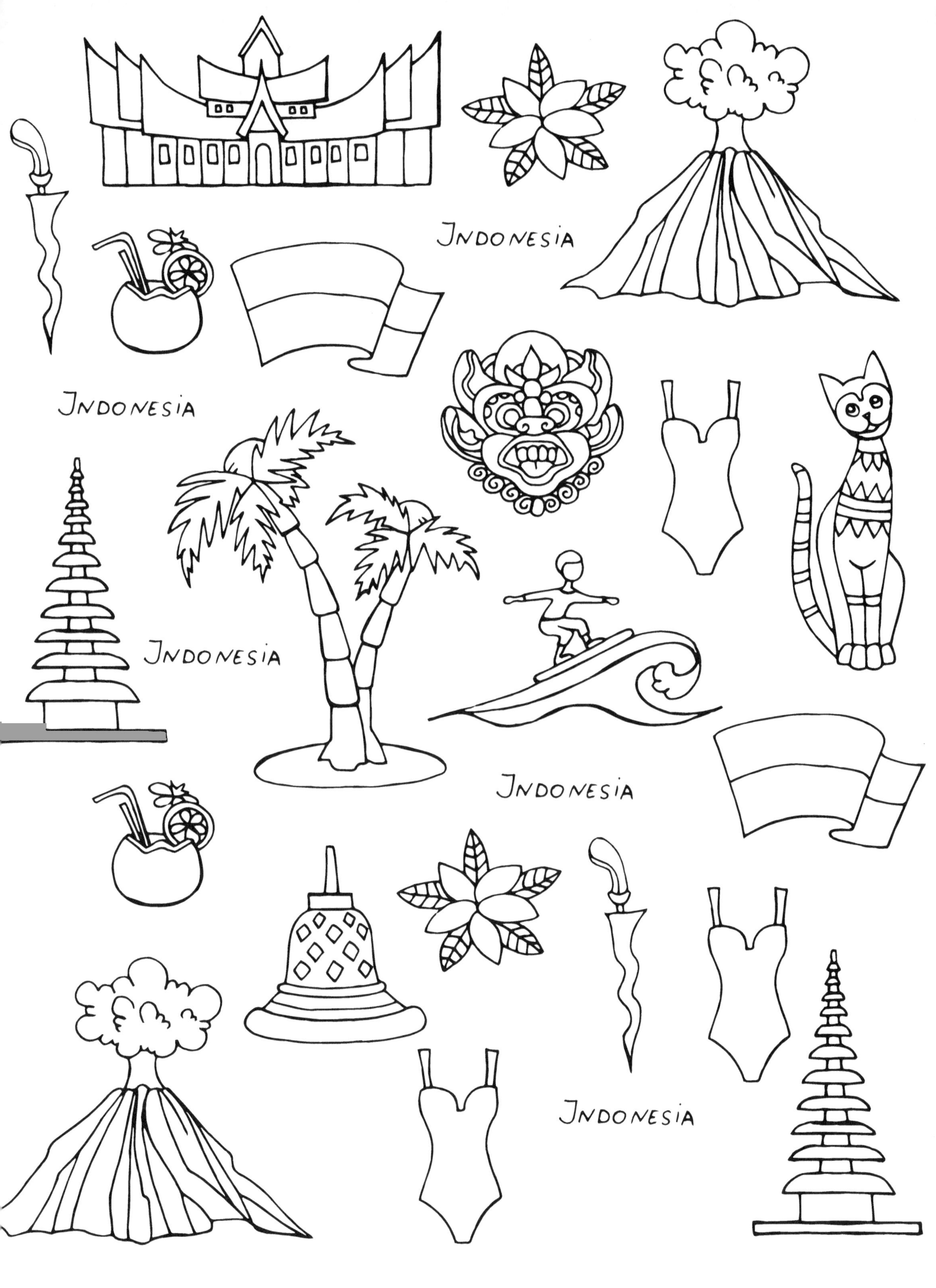
INDONESIA
INDONESIA
INDONESIA
INDONESIA
INDONESIA

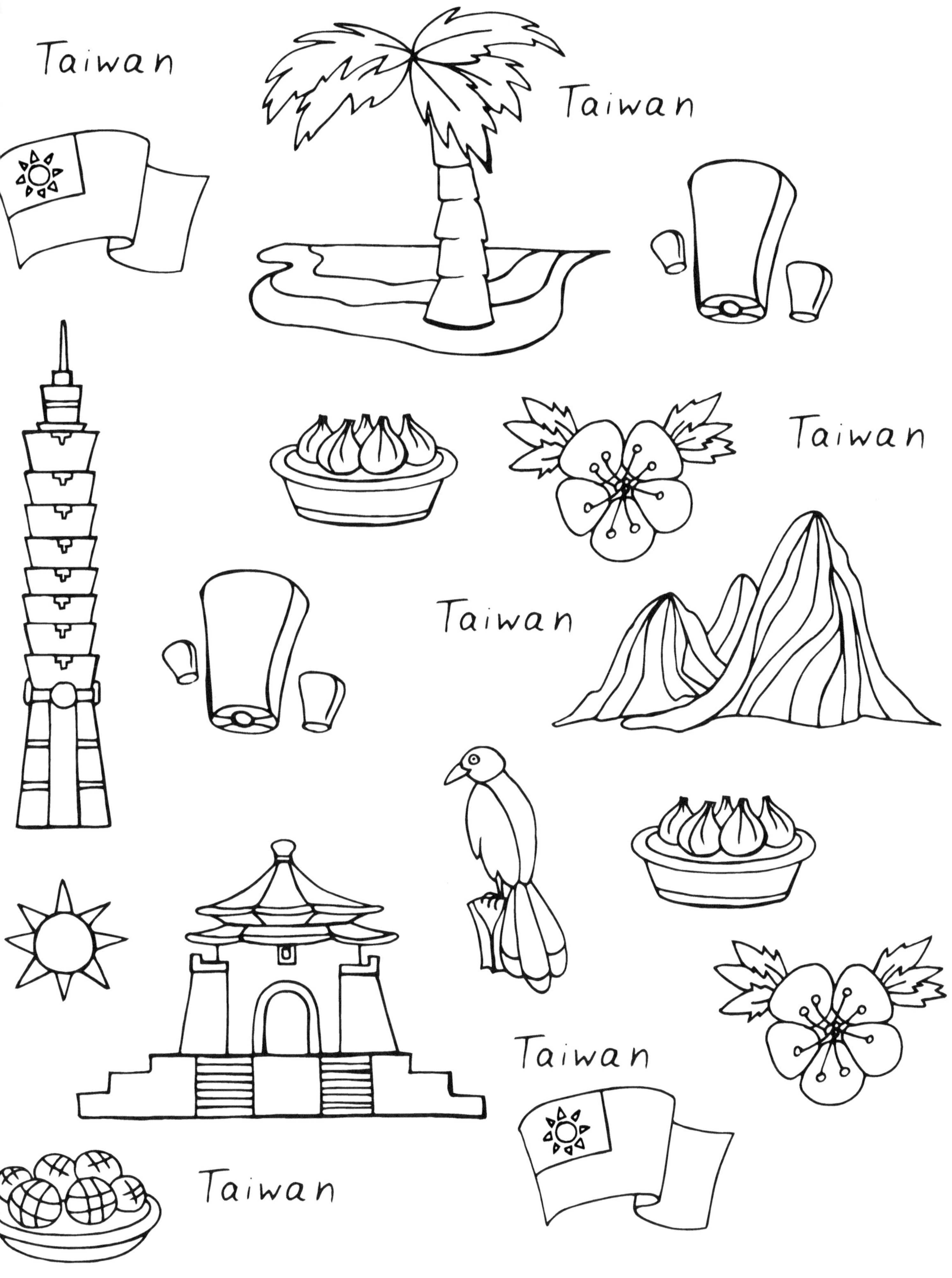
Taiwan
Taiwan
Taiwan
Taiwan
Taiwan
Taiwan

MAP
Travel
Ticket

www.ingramcontent.com/pod-product-compliance
Lightning Source LLC
LaVergne TN
LVHW061256100826
845148LV00008B/1143

9781785951510